My First Flower Garden

Designed and Illustrated
by Ley Honor Roberts

eden project

Contents

Getting started

Jolly, orange nasturtiums are really easy to grow. They will trail nicely from a big pot, a window box or a hanging basket, or brighten up a sunny flowerbed. Start them early indoors in small containers or wait until it's warmer and sow them straight outside. Here's what you will need:

A sunny patch of earth

Or 2 or 3 big containers are good if you don't have a garden.

4

Seed pots

All these things make good first plant pots for seeds. Solid containers need drainage holes in the bottom.(Ask for adult help with this.)

Water
Rainwater is best, but tap water will do.

Nasturtium seeds look like little brains.

Seed compost

Available in bags from supermarkets and garages as well as garden centres. Peat-free is best.

Gro-bags are a cheap way of buying seed compost.

Patience

The nasturtiums will take about 8 weeks to get from seed to flower. Keep a diary to see how they grow each day.

Sowing your nasturtium seeds

The best time to sow

The best time to sow is March and April indoors, or May and June outside. After midsummer, the days get shorter and the plants don't have time to reach their full height and make flowers before autumn.

		planting time			midsummer		flowering time				
Jan	Feb	Mar	Apr	May	Jun	Jul	Aug	Sep	Oct	Nov	Dec

what to do

1. **Either** fill your containers with seed compost.

Gardening is a good excuse to get your hands muddy!

OR ...
Wait until it's warmer and find a sunny spot in the garden. Clear away any weeds and stones.

2. Water the seed compost (in the pots) or the soil (in the flowerbed). Make sure it is moist but not too wet – like a squeezed-out sponge.

3. Plant your seeds 15 cms apart at twice their own depth.

If you are starting them off in egg boxes, put one in each section.

4. Cover the seeds with seed compost (if they're in pots) or earth (if they're in a flowerbed).

Like us, seeds need water, air and food to grow.
Your nasturtium seeds get their water and air from the soil,
and food from inside their seed coats (which is why they are quite big).
When the shoots appear above the soil, they need light too.

From seeds to seedlings

Sunlight

Once your nasturtium seeds have sprouted, make sure they have plenty of sun. If they are in pots, move them into the sunshine.

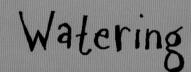

Watering

Water the seedlings so the soil or compost stays damp. That might not be every day.

If it is too wet, your seedlings will drown because they can't breathe.

If it is too dry, the seedlings could die of thirst.

If the seedlings are strong and look good, you've got the right balance.

Potting on

Once nasturtium seedlings have four little
leaves they will need more room to grow if they are in small pots.
Now is the time to plant them in bigger containers, or in the garden (if you
didn't sow the seeds outside in the first place).

Turn to the next page to find out how to plant out seedlings.

Planting out your seedlings

How to plant out seedlings from small pots

Turn the pot upside down and gently pull it off the plant.
Try to keep as much soil on the roots as possible. Dig a hole and plant the seedling in the soil at the same depth as it was in the compost. Press it in with your fingers but be careful not to squash the stem – this is like the plant's drinking straw for sucking up water up from the soil.

Biodegradable seed pots

Seedlings in cardboard containers like egg boxes can stay in them, because the cardboard will rot. Separate the sections and tear the edges a bit before putting them in the earth.

Interesting pots

I've planted two nasturtium seedlings in this piece of old guttering.

Two or three seedlings will grow big enough to fill a hanging basket.

Friends and Foes

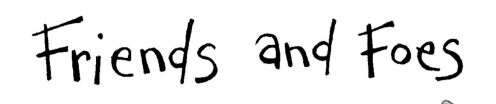

Caterpillars Some butterflies like to lay their eggs under nasturtium leaves. When the eggs hatch, hundreds of tiny caterpillars can munch their way through them. Check the leaves daily and remove the caterpillars.

Aphids Blackfly are aphids that love nasturtiums. Get rid of these pests by watering the plants with a weak solution of eco washing-up liquid. Water them with a weak solution of liquid seaweed (from a garden centre) as a tonic to help them get better. Ask an adult to help you with this.

Ladybirds are really good for your nasturtiums because they love to eat aphids. If you see any ladybirds in your garden, catch them very carefully and put them on your plants.

Worms Be gentle with worms – unlike slugs and snails, they are gardeners' friends, helping to dig the soil as they make channels through it, and helping to feed it with their poo!

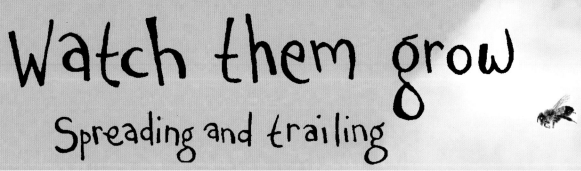

Watch them grow
Spreading and trailing

Your nasturtium plants will soon spread to fill the space. As they get more and more umbrella-like leaves they will start to trail down from hanging baskets and other containers.

Soon they will be covered with bright orange flowers that close up at night. Look for dewdrops in the middle of the leaves first thing in the morning after a clear night.

Bees

The bright flowers will attract honey bees, who come to collect sweet nectar and pollen.

Watering

Water your nasturtiums if it doesn't rain.
Make sure the water goes down into the soil.
Remember that plants in pots dry out very fast.

If you go away on holiday, ask someone to water them for you.

A plant you can eat

Leaves

Another name for nasturtiums is summer watercress.
Try nibbling a young leaf. It tastes quite hot, like watercress.
You can add a few to your salad or sandwich. A nasturtium
leaf contains ten times more Vitamin C than a lettuce leaf.

Flowers

Nasturtium flowers grow in lots of different shades of yellow, orange and red.

You can eat the flowers too!
They look lovely in a green salad.

Nasturtium seeds

When the flowers are over, look for the round seeds. You can dry these by leaving them on a sunny windowsill for a couple of weeks. Put them in the packet ready to plant next year. If you're really keen, you can pickle the seeds in vinegar. They taste like capers.

NASTURTIUMS
eden project 20 Double Gleam seeds

Make a gift

A pot or a hanging basket of nasturtiums would make a perfect present for the person who gave you this book.

Did you know?

What's in a name?

The name nasturtium comes from the Latin *nasturcium* from *nasus torquere*, meaning 'twisted nose' – because that's what you do when you taste its peppery leaves!

Nasturtium is actually the botanical name for watercress. Nasturtiums were originally known as Indian cress, but the nasturtium tag stuck as the common name for our orange flowers.

Trophy flowers

The botanical name for nasturtium is *Tropaeolum majus*. It was named by the botanist Carl Linnaeus after the Greek word for 'trophy', because the flower reminded him of a classical trophy with round shields and golden helmets.

All the way from Peru

Nasturtiums are native to Peru. They were introduced into European gardens in the seventeenth century.

Getting started

Tall sunflowers are fun to grow. Even though they are going to grow taller than you, they will work just as well in a big pot or window box as in a flower bed. You can start them off in small containers where you can keep an eye on them if you want to. Here's what you will need:

Some space in a sunny flower bed

Or 2 or 3 big containers are good if you don't have a garden.

Containers

Solid containers need drainage holes in the bottom. (Ask for adult help with this.)

Seed pots

All these things make good first plant pots for seeds.

Water Rainwater is best, but tap water will do.

Sticks

Bought from the garden centre (say you want them for sunflowers), or suitable ones that you pick up in the garden.

Seed compost

Sunflower seeds are big and stripy.

Available in bags from supermarkets and garages as well as garden centres. Peat-free is best.

Gro-bags are a cheap way of buying seed compost.

Patience

The sunflowers will take about 12 weeks to get from seed to flower. Keep a diary to see how they grow each day.

Sowing your sunflower seeds

The best time to sow

The best time to sow is between April and July.
After midsummer, the days get shorter and the plants don't have time to grow up and make flowers before the cooler days of autumn set in.

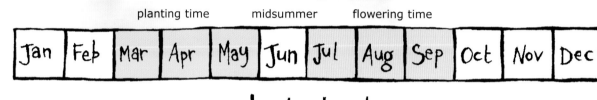

			planting time		midsummer		flowering time				
Jan	Feb	Mar	Apr	May	Jun	Jul	Aug	Sep	Oct	Nov	Dec

what to do

1. **Either** find a sunny spot in the garden, preferably sheltered by a fence or a wall. Clear away any weeds and stones.

OR ...
Fill your containers with seed compost.

Don't worry about getting your hands dirty!

2. Water the soil (in the flower bed) or the seed compost (in the pots). Make sure it is moist but not too wet – like a squeezed-out sponge.

3. Plant your seeds 30 cms apart at twice their own depth.

I'm planting my seeds in small plant pots.

If you are starting them off in smaller pots, put one or two seeds in each (depending on the size of the pot).

4. Cover the seeds with soil (in the garden) or seed compost (in pots).

Like us, seeds need water, air and food to grow.
Your sunflower seeds get their water and air from the soil and food from inside their seed coats (which is why they are quite big).
When the shoots appear above the soil, they need light too.

From seeds to seedlings

Sunlight

Once your sunflower seeds have sprouted,
make sure they have plenty of sun.
If they are in pots, move them into the sunshine.

Watering

Water the seedlings so the soil or compost stays damp.
That might not be every day.
If it is too wet, your seedlings will drown because they can't breathe.
If it is too dry, the seedlings could die of thirst.
If the seedlings are strong and look good, you've got the right balance.

The first tiny leaves will appear 1-2 weeks after you plant the seeds.

potting on

Once sunflower seedlings have four little leaves they will need more room to grow if they are in small pots.

Now is the time to plant them in bigger containers, or in the garden (if you didn't sow the seeds outside in the first place).

Turn to the next page to find out how to plant out seedlings.

Planting out your seedlings

How to plant out seedlings from small pots

Turn the pot upside down and gently pull it off the plant, trying to keep as much soil on the roots as possible.

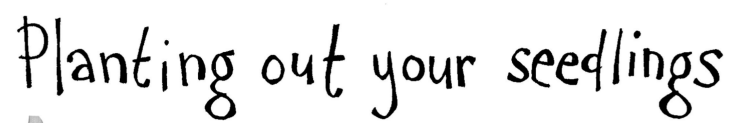

Look at these roots! These plants need more room to grow.

Dig a hole about the same size as the plant pot and plant the seedlings in the soil at the same depth as they were in the compost. Press them in with your fingers but be careful not to squash the stem – this is like the plant's drinking straw for sucking up water up from the soil.

Thinning out

If your seedlings are already growing in a big container or a flowerbed, and they look a bit overcrowded, you could pull out the spindly ones to give the strong ones more room to grow.

Slugs and snails

Slugs and snails can munch through your seedlings overnight and ruin all your hard work. Depending on the sort of person you are, you can

DISCOURAGE THEM

by making barriers from hair cuttings, sand or broken-up eggshells.

TRAP THEM

under upside-down grapefruit halves. They will hide there.

KILL THEM

in a jar or saucer of beer. They will fall in and drown.

Cats

Cats can sometimes be a nuisance in gardens if they use your flower bed as a loo. A plastic lemonade bottle filled with water reflects the light and can discourage them.

Watering

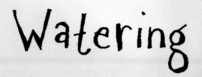

Water your sunflowers if it doesn't rain.
Make sure the water goes down into the soil.
Remember that plants in pots dry out very fast.

Sunflower seeds

As the plant finishes flowering, you will see the seeds forming in the middle of the flower head. Hang the flowerheads upside down to dry. Here are some ways you can use your sunflower seeds:

Make necklaces and bracelets. You'll need a sharp needle and strong thread, so ask for adult help.

Make a picture. You could use other parts of the dried flowerhead as well.

Birds and pet hamsters love sunflower seeds.

I like to eat sunflower seeds that have been shelled and roasted.

SUNFLOWERS
eden project   20 Moonwalker seeds

Save some in the packet to plant next year.

Useful seeds

Sunflower seeds are squeezed to make oil which is used for frying chips and turning into margarine, as well as for lubricating racing car engines.

Facts to quiz your friends on

Q What is the only major food crop to originate in North America?
Q What plant is capable of sucking up radioactivity?
Q Which flowers famously inspired the painter Van Gogh?
Q What is Russia's biggest crop?

The answer to all of these questions is SUNFLOWERS! What amazing plants!

Follow the sun

Sunflowers are 'heliotropic', which means that they turn their heads to follow the sun during the course of the day. That's why the French call the sunflower a 'tournesol'.

Fibonacci

Leonardo Fibonacci was an Italian mathematician, born around 1170. One of the many clever things he did was to see that the numbers occurring in a particular sequence - where each number is the sum of the two previous ones, eg 1 1 2 3 5 8 13 21 34 etc - apply to many forms in nature.

The spiral patterns in the sunflower seedheads follow the patterns of the Fibonacci sequence. This ensures that the flower packs in as many seeds as possible.

Getting started

Everybody loves sweet peas, with their pretty colours and gorgeous scent. People will think that you are very clever to grow your own. In fact, sweet peas are not hard to grow, and will do as well on a windowsill as in a garden. Here is what you will need to get started:

Seed compost

Available in bags from supermarkets and garages as well as garden centres. Peat-free is best.

Don't use potting compost - it's too rich for your seeds.

Gro-bags are a cheap way of buying seed compost.

Sticks

Bought from the garden centre (ask for pea sticks), or suitable ones that you pick up in the garden.

Seed pots

All these things make good plant pots for seeds.

Half a kitchen roll tube filled with damp soil works well for sweet peas.

Solid containers need drainage holes in the bottom. (Ask for adult help with this.)

Soak the seeds overnight for best results.

Water Rainwater is best, but tap water will do.

Patience The sweet peas will take about 12 weeks to get from seed to flower. Keep a diary to see how they grow each day.

Sowing your sweet pea seeds

The best time to sow

The best time to sow is between March and midsummer. After midsummer, the days get shorter and the plants don't have time to grow up and make flowers before the cooler days of autumn set in. You can also plant them in September and keep them over winter in a light, sheltered spot.

planting time   midsummer   flowering time

Jan	Feb	Mar	Apr	May	Jun	Jul	Aug	Sep	Oct	Nov	Dec

what to do

I'm planting my seeds in fibre pots in a seed tray.

1. Fill your containers with soil. Don't worry about getting your hands dirty!

2. Water the soil. Make sure that it is moist but not too wet – like a squeezed-out sponge.

3. Plant one seed in each fibre pot or section of an egg box, or one in each half of the cardboard tube. In a big container plant the seeds about 5cms apart.

Plant your seeds at twice their own depth.

Sweet pea seeds don't need light at first but the temperature needs to be above 6°c.

4. Cover the seeds with soil.

Like us, sweet peas need water, air and food to grow. The sweet pea seeds get their water from the soil and food from inside their seed coats (which is why they are quite big). As they push above the soil they need light too, and eventually more food from their compost.

From seeds to seedlings

Sunlight

As soon as your seeds start to sprout, put them in a sunny place. Turn each container every day so the seedlings don't bend one way towards the sun.

Watering

Water the seedlings so the compost stays damp. That might not be every day.
If the container is dripping, your seedlings will drown because they can't breathe.
If the compost is too dry the seedlings will die of thirst.
If they are nice and green and look good, you've got the right balance.

Talk to your seedlings! Encourage them.

Slugs and snails

Look out for slugs and snails – they'll be hiding in damp and dark places, such as under the pots. Get rid of them.

Preparing the ground for planting

(See the next page if you are growing your sweetpeas in big containers.)

1. Find a sunny spot.

While your seedlings are growing is the time to do this.

2. Remove the stones and big weeds.

3. Fork the soil over. Be gentle with worms – unlike slugs and snails, they are gardeners' friends, helping to dig the soil as they make channels through it, and helping to feed it with their poo!

Planting out your seedlings

In the garden

Remove seedlings from their small pots or tray.
Be very careful when you pull them up so as to not snap the roots.
Gently remove from the container, trying to keep as much soil
around the roots as possible.

I can put this seedling in the ground in its fibre pot because it rots, so do eggboxes and cardboard tubes. You might need to shred them a bit first.

Try 'puddling in'

Make a little hole and fill it with water. Let the water drain away before planting the seedling.

Plant the seedlings in the soil

Plant them at the same depth as they were in the compost.
Press them in with your fingers but be careful not to squash the stem
—this is the plant's drinking straw for sucking up water from the soil.

In large containers

You don't have to have a big garden to grow Sweet peas. You can grow them in a large pot or bucket or even in a window box.

Fill your container with compost (don't forget the holes in the bottom) and plant your seedlings in the same way.

Watering

Water your plants if it doesn't rain.
Make sure the water goes down into the soil.
Remember that plants in pots dry out very fast.

Sticks

Put a stick beside each seedling now. Put something on the end of the stick to protect your eyes, such as a bottle top, plasticine, tennis ball or a rubber glove.

Caring for your sweet pea plants

Climbing frames

Here are some ways of supporting them if you have more room outside.
Make climbing frames for your plants from pea sticks, or trellis.

A wigwam is a good shape for a frame, whether you are growing your sweet peas in the soil or in a pot. Push your sticks into the ground in a circle and tie them together at the top.

How sweet peas climb

Sweet peas have long tendrils that wrap around anything they can find to pull the plant upwards towards the sun.

If you have lots of room in your garden you could make a tent-shape frame from bamboos or sticks from the garden.

When your sweet peas have grown you will have a beautiful and fragrant den to hide in.

 # Slugs and snails

Slugs and snails can munch through your seedlings overnight and ruin all your hard work. Depending on the sort of person you are, you can

DISCOURAGE THEM

by making barriers from hair cuttings, sand or broken-up eggshells.

TRAP THEM

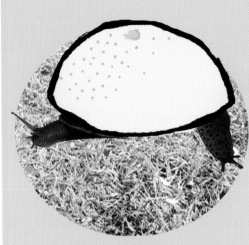

under upside-down grapefruit halves. They will hide there.

KILL THEM

in a jar or saucer of beer. They will fall in and drown.

More pests

APHIDS suck sap and spread disease, Get rid of these pests by watering the plants with a weak solution of eco washing-up liquid. Water them with a weak solution of liquid seaweed (from a garden centre) as a tonic to help them get better. Ask an adult to help you with this.

Lovely scented sweet peas

What to do with the flowers

keep cutting the flowers – this encourages the plant to grow more. Pick off any dead flowers.

Make a gift

Tie a nice bunch with ribbon as a gift for the donor of this book!

Grow again

SWEET PEAS
eden project 20 Fragrantissima seeds

Save some seeds for next year. Leave them on a sunny windowsill for a couple of weeks to dry out.

Perfume and pot pourri

Use petals and water to make scented flower water.

Hang some bunches up to dry and use the dried petals for scented pot pourri.

pretty pictures

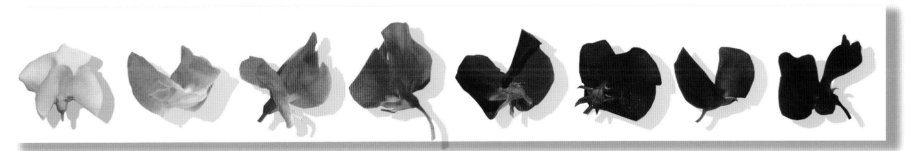

Make a colour palette from the different coloured flowers you have grown.
Make a picture from them. You could press it by covering it
with paper and putting it inside a heavy book for a couple of weeks.

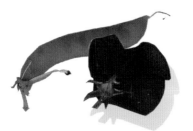

Did you Know?

Meet the family

The pea family is large and varied. It contains:

annuals (that live for one year) – like sweet peas,
perennials (that live for several years) – like lupins,
vegetables – like runner beans,
shrubs – like gorse,
trees – like highly poisonous laburnum.

lupins

runner beans

gorse

laburnum

Most of them are easy to spot, because they have pods, flowers shaped like sweet peas, and finely-divided leaves.

Making protein from fresh air

Protein plants

Sweet peas are poisonous, but there are plenty of plants in this family that we eat all the time, such as lentils, peas, beans and chick peas. They are called pulses and they are useful in non-meat diets because they contain protein.

Friendly bacteria

Plants in this family make their own protein with the help of some friendly bacteria that live in their roots and feed on the sugars made by the plant. The bacteria mix nitrogen from the air (that reaches them through holes in the soil) with the sugars to make protein.

That's good for us, because even though the air we breathe is 78% nitrogen, we can't convert it into protein ourselves. We have to depend on the bacteria for that.

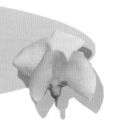

The Eden Project brings plants and people together.
It is dedicated to developing a greater understanding
of our shared global garden, encouraging us to respect
plants and protect them.

MY FIRST FLOWER GARDEN
AN EDEN PROJECT BOOK 978 1 84941500 2
Published in Great Britain by Eden Project Books,
an imprint of Transworld Publishers
A Random House Group Company
This book was originally published as three separate editions, *Grow Your Own Nasturtiums*, 2005; *Grow Your Own Sunflowers*, 2005;
and *Grow Your Own Sweet Peas*, 2006
This edition published 2011
1 3 5 7 9 10 8 6 4 2
Text copyright © The Eden Project, 2005 and 2006
Illustrations copyright © Ley Honor Roberts, 2005 and 2006
The right of The Eden Project and Ley Honor Roberts to be identified as the author and illustrator of this work has been
asserted in accordance with the Copyrights, Designs and Patents Act 1988.
All rights reserved.
TRANSWORLD PUBLISHERS
61-63 Uxbridge Road, London, W5 5SA
www.**edenproject**.co.uk
www.**kids**at**randomhouse**.co.uk
Addresses for companies within The Random House Group Limited can be found at: www.randomhouse.co.uk/offices.htm
THE RANDOM HOUSE GROUP Limited Reg. No. 954009
A CIP record for this book is available from the British Library.
The Eden Project is owned by the Eden Trust, a registered charity.
Eden Project, Bodelva, St Austell, Cornwall PL24 2SG
Printed and bound in China